W9-CNW-254

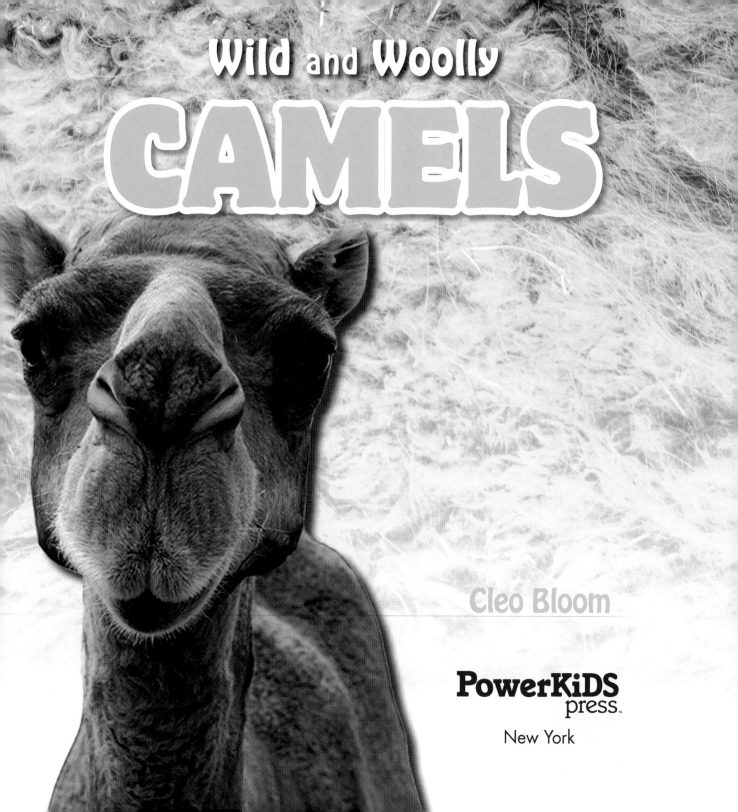

Wild and Woolly
CAMELS

Cleo Bloom

PowerKiDS
press™

New York

Published in 2018 by The Rosen Publishing Group, Inc.
29 East 21st Street, New York, NY 10010

First Edition

Editor: Theresa Morlock
Book Design: Rachel Rising

Photo Credits: Cover, p. 1 iStockphoto.com/jane; Cover (background) Chris Garlotta/EyeEm/Getty Images; Cover (texture) pp. 1,3, 4, 6, 7, 8, 9, 10, 12, 16, 18, 20, 22, 23, 24 panyajampatong/Shutterstock.com; p. 4 Artorn Thongtukit/Shutterstock.com; p. 5 happystock/Shutterstock.com; p. 6 Wolfgang Zwanzger/Shutterstock.com; pp. 7, 11 aleksander hunta/Shutterstock.com; p. 8 Oprea George/Shutterstock.com; p. 9 seeyah panwan/Shutterstock.com; p. 13 David Steele/Shutterstock.com; p. 14 Lotus_studio/Shutterstock.com; p. 15 Aloyzas Nomeika/Shutterstock.com; p. 16 Ranglen/Shutterstock.com; p. 17 MehmetO/Shutterstock.com;p.18 Zdenek Adamec/Shutterstock.com; p. 19 Nadya Korobkova/Shutterstock.com; p. 20 Denis Selivanov/Shutterstock.com; p. 21 shapicingvar/Shutterstock.com; p. 22 schankz/Shutterstock.com.

Library of Congress Cataloging-in-Publication Data

Names: Bloom, Cleo, author.
Title: Camels / Cleo Bloom.
Description: New York : PowerKids Press, [2018] | Series: Wild and woolly |
  Includes index.
Identifiers: LCCN 2017030197| ISBN 9781538325278 (library bound) | ISBN
  9781538325971 (pbk.) | ISBN 9781538325988 (6 pack)
Subjects: LCSH: Camels–Juvenile literature.
Classification: LCC QL737.U54 B58 2018 | DDC 599.63/62–dc23
LC record available at https://lccn.loc.gov/2017030197

Manufactured in the United States of America

CPSIA Compliance Information: Batch #BW18PK: For Further Information contact Rosen Publishing, New York, New York at 1-800-237-9932

CONTENTS

Ships of the Desert

More than 3,000 years ago, people living throughout the grasslands and deserts of Africa and Asia **domesticated** camels. Since that time, people have kept these tall, **majestic** creatures as livestock. People ride camels, use them to carry heavy loads, eat their meat, and drink their milk.

One of the most important **resources** that camels offer is their hair. Camel hair is a beautiful light brown color. It's used to make very warm, long-lasting clothing that's comfortable to wear.

In some African cultures, people **traditionally** measured their wealth by the amount of camels they owned.

One Hump or Two?

There are two main species, or kinds, of camels. You can tell them apart based on their humps. Bactrian camels have two humps on their back. Arabian camels, also called dromedaries, only have one hump.

Camels' humps store fat. Camels use this stored fat as energy. Stored fat can also be turned into water. An Arabian camel's hump holds up to 80 pounds (36.3 kg) of fat! After the camel uses its stored fat, the hump becomes floppy.

Arabian

6

Bactrian

Wild Bactrian camels are considered a critically endangered species. That means they are at a very high risk of dying out completely.

Fuzzy Features

Today, the only nondomesticated camels are wild Bactrian camels. There are less than 400 wild Bactrian camels left. They live in the Gobi Desert in Mongolia and China.

Life in the Desert

Camels live in the deserts and grasslands of Africa and Asia. Some camels now also live in Australia.

Thanks to the stored fat in their humps, camels can travel up to 100 miles (160.9 km) in the desert without water. When they do come across water, they can drink up to 30 gallons (113.6 L) in just 13 minutes!

Camels are herbivores, which means they only eat plants. Camels can survive on the water from plants alone for several weeks during the winter.

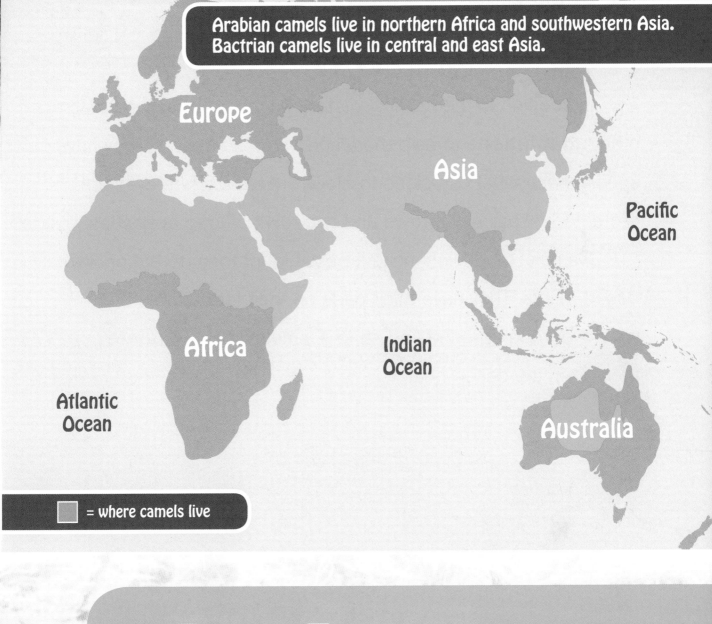

Arabian camels live in northern Africa and southwestern Asia. Bactrian camels live in central and east Asia.

Europe

Asia

Pacific Ocean

Africa

Indian Ocean

Atlantic Ocean

Australia

= where camels live

Fuzzy Features

Baby camels are born without humps.

9

Desert Adaptations

In addition to their ability to store fat, camels have several other **adaptations** to help them survive in the desert. They have special noses that can close to block out sand. Their eyes are protected by hairy eyebrows and two rows of long eyelashes.

Camels' rough lips make it possible for them to eat prickly desert plants. They have thick pads on their feet to help them walk over rough ground and sand. Camels' coats **insulate** them from the desert heat.

Fuzzy Features

Camels almost never sweat! Their bodies preserve as much water as possible.

Temperatures in the desert can range from -20° Fahrenheit (-28.9° Celsius) to over 100° Fahrenheit (37.8° Celsius). Bactrian camels have thick coats to keep them warm. They shed this coat seasonally.

11

A Caravan of Camels

A group of camels is called a caravan or a flock. In the wild, caravans are made up of many females and one male.

Camels are mammals. They give birth to one baby at a time. Baby camels are called calves. They're born with their eyes open and can run the same day they're born. Calves stay with their mothers for several years.

Camels reach adulthood when they're about five years old. They can live for up to 50 years.

Fuzzy Features

Lions aren't the only animals that roar! Did you know that camels also make a loud noise called a roar?

Adult camels are about 7 feet (2.1 m) tall at the hump. Arabian camels weigh up to 1,600 pounds (725 kg) and Bactrian camels weigh up to 1,800 pounds (816.5 kg).

13

Beasts of Burden

One of the main uses of domesticated camels is as transportation. An adult male camel can carry 440 pounds (200 kg) on its back for a short period of time.

Camels can travel up to 25 miles (40.2 km) a day while carrying heavy loads of up to 200 pounds (90.7 kg) on their back! In short bursts, camels can run at speeds up to 40 miles (64.4 km) per hour. Over longer distances, their average speed is about 25 miles (40.2 km) per hour.

Camel racing is a popular sport in several countries in the Middle East.

15

Meat and Milk

Like cows, camels are kept for their meat and milk. Camels can produce up to 6 quarts (5.7 L) of milk per day. Camel milk is very healthy for people to drink. It can also be made into cheese and yogurt.

Although camel meat is not very popular in the United States, it is a key product in other parts of the world. In Australia, there is a large population of **feral** camels. To get rid of these camels, Australians have begun to sell their meat.

← camel dung

Fuzzy Features

People use camel droppings, called dung, as **fuel**. The dung is dried and burned.

In this picture, a woman in Turkey is collecting camel milk in a bucket.

17

Camel Hair

Bactrian camels are kept for their warm, golden brown hair. Camels have an outer coat of **coarse** hair and an undercoat of soft hair. The undercoat is collected and made into **textiles**.

Camels shed their hair naturally during the late spring and early summer. It's during this time that the hair is collected. Since the outer coat and undercoat shed at the same time, people use combs to sort the hairs. One camel can produce 17.6 to 22 pounds (8 to 10 kg) of hair per year.

camel wool rug

Camel hair is used to make jackets, skirts, gloves, hats, scarves, and more.

19

Processing the Hair

Camel hair goes through several steps before being made into textiles. After hair is sorted, it's washed to remove any dirt. The sorted and washed hair then goes through a process called dehairing. During dehairing, more coarse hairs are removed, leaving behind only the softest pieces. Only about 30 percent of this hair is judged good enough for fabric making.

Next, the hair can be spun into yarn. The process by which yarn is made into textiles is called weaving.

camel yarn ⟶

Today, China is the leading producer
of camel-hair products.

21

Amazing Animals

With their long, powerful legs, unusual humps, and gentle brown eyes, camels are a sight to see! Many people believe camels to be a **symbol** of patience and strength.

Camels continue to be an important resource today. They provide milk and meat for people to eat, transportation for people and goods, and strong hair that can be made into textiles. These cool creatures are some of the most useful livestock animals in the world, and they've been working with humans for over 3,000 years.

GLOSSARY

adaptation: A change in a living thing to help it survive better in its environment.

coarse: Rough or wiry.

domesticate: To breed and raise animals for use by people.

feral: Used to refer to an animal that used to live with humans but has gone back to the wild.

fuel: Something used to make energy, warmth, or power.

insulate: To prevent the passage of heat into or out of something.

majestic: Impressive or grand.

resource: Something that can be used.

symbol: Something that stands for something else.

textile: A kind of cloth that is woven or knit.

traditionally: Following what's been done for a long time.

INDEX

WEBSITES

Due to the changing nature of Internet links, PowerKids Press has developed an online list of websites related to the subject of this book. This site is updated regularly. Please use this link to access the list: www.powerkidslinks.com/wandw/camel